STAND UP SPEAK OUT

LGBTQ+ RIGHTS

Virginia Loh-Hagan

1

45TH PARALLEL PRESS

Published in the United States of America by Cherry Lake Publishing Group
Ann Arbor, Michigan
www.cherrylakepublishing.com

Reading Adviser: Beth Walker Gambro, MS, Ed., Reading Consultant, Yorkville, IL
Content Adviser: Lauren Fisher
Book Designer: Jen Wahi

45th Parallel Press is an imprint of Cherry Lake Publishing Group.

Library of Congress Cataloging-in-Publication Data

Names: Loh-Hagan, Virginia, author.
Title: LGBTQ+ rights / by Virginia Loh-Hagan.
Other titles: Lesbian, gay, bisexual, transgender, queer+ rights
Description: Ann Arbor, Michigan : Cherry Lake Publishing, 2021. | Series: Stand up, speak out | Includes index.
Identifiers: LCCN 2021004971 (print) | LCCN 2021004972 (ebook) | ISBN 9781534187542 (hardcover) | ISBN 9781534188945 (paperback) | ISBN 9781534190344 (pdf) | ISBN 9781534191747 (ebook)
Subjects: LCSH: Sexual minorities–Political activity–Juvenile literature. | Sexual minorities–Civil rights–Juvenile literature.
Classification: LCC HQ76.5 .L64 2021 (print) | LCC HQ76.5 (ebook) | DDC 306.76–dc23
LC record available at https://lccn.loc.gov/2021004971
LC ebook record available at https://lccn.loc.gov/2021004972

Printed in the United States of America
Corporate Graphics

About the Author:

Dr. Virginia Loh-Hagan (she/her/hers) is an author, university professor, and former classroom teacher. She's currently the Director of the Asian Pacific Islander Desi American Resource Center at San Diego State University. She lives in San Diego with her very tall husband and very naughty dogs. She dedicates this book to her students and readers who identify as LGBTQ+. She sees you.

TABLE OF CONTENTS

INTRODUCTION:
What Is LGBTQ+ Activism?. 5

CHAPTER 1:
End Violence and Celebrate Pride 9

CHAPTER 2:
Use Pronouns 15

CHAPTER 3:
Support Gender-Neutral Bathrooms 21

CHAPTER 4:
Fight for Same-Sex Marriage 27

Glossary 32

Learn More! 32

Index. 32

Activists often work as a group. They have power in numbers.

WHAT IS LGBTQ+ ACTIVISM?

Everyone has the power to make our world a better place. A person just has to act. **Activists** fight for change. They want **justice**. Justice is upholding what is right. Activists help others.

There are all types of love. There are all types of people. People have the right to be who they want to be. Many activists feel strongly about LGBTQ+ rights. LGBTQ+ refers to several identities. A woman who loves a woman may identify as a **lesbian**. People who love people of the same sex may identify as **gay**. A person who loves both men and women might identity as bisexual. **Transgender** describes people whose identity and gender expression differs from the sex they were assigned at birth. **Queer** is a word that describes other identities beyond straight and **cisgender**. Cisgender means having your sex at birth match your gender identity. Lesbian, gay, bisexual, and transgender people may all identify with queer. The plus sign means there are more identities.

In this book, we share examples of LGBTQ+ issues and actions. We also share tips for how to engage. Your activist journey starts here!

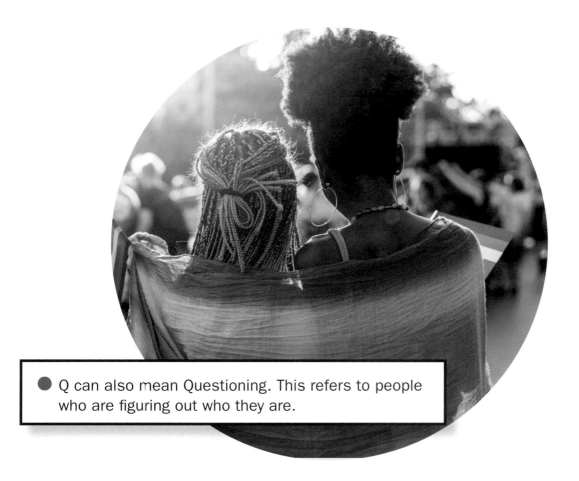

Q can also mean Questioning. This refers to people who are figuring out who they are.

GET STARTED

Community service is about helping others. It's about creating a kinder world. Activism goes beyond service. It's about making a fairer and more just world. It involves acting and fighting for change. Choose to be an activist!

○ **Focus on your cause!** In addition to the topics covered in this book, there are many others. Other examples include supporting LGBTQ+ persons in the military and ending hate crimes.

○ **Do your research!** Learn all you can about the cause. Learn about the history. Learn from other activists.

○ **Make a plan!** Get organized.

○ **Make it happen!** Act! There are many ways to act. Activists write letters. They write petitions. They protest. They march in the streets. They ban or **boycott**. Boycott means to avoid or not buy something as a protest. They perform art to make people aware. They post to social media. They fight to change laws. They organize sit-in events. They participate in demonstrations and **strikes**. During strikes, people protest by refusing to do something, such as work.

● LGBTQ+ activist groups want to provide safe spaces for the LGBTQ+ community.

CHAPTER 1

END VIOLENCE AND CELEBRATE PRIDE

Folks who identify as LGBTQ+ should have the same rights as everyone else. But they don't. Their love is even illegal in some countries. They can be arrested. Lebanon is one of the countries where LGBTQ+ people can be punished. Tarek Zeidan leads a group called Helem. This is the first LGBTQ+ rights group in the Arab world. Helem gets people out of jail. Its members provide food and other services.

LGBTQ+ folks have been unfairly treated. Some have been victims of hate crimes. Some have been rejected by their families. Some hide who they are out of fear. LGBTQ+ activists fight to change this. LGBTQ+ folks should have the right to love who they love. They should be able to

GET INSPIRED

BY PIONEERS IN LGBTQ+ RIGHTS ACTIVISM!

○ **Harvey Milk** made U.S. history in 1977. He became the first openly gay person to be an elected official. He united LGBTQ+ business leaders. He founded the San Francisco Gay Democratic Club. He fought to ban discrimination against LGBTQ+ folks. He was killed in 1978. His birthday, May 22, is celebrated as Harvey Milk Day.

○ **Megan Rapinoe** is a professional soccer player. She is the captain of the United States' national team. She has won several gold medals. She is an activist. She identifies as gay and lesbian. She supports equal rights. She is a member of Athlete Ally. It's an organization that seeks to provide equal opportunities in sports to LGBTQ+ folks.

○ **Marsha P. Johnson** and **Sylvia Rivera** were transgender activists. They were at the Stonewall riots. They resisted. They organized protests. They opened a shelter for homeless LGBTQ+ youth. In 2018, the city of New York announced its plan for statues honoring Johnson and Rivera.

At Pride events, there are parades and parties. People wear colorful outfits.

identify the way they feel on the inside. No one should be denied the right to be proud.

Geena Rocero is a model. Rocero came out during a TED Talk. Coming out means sharing one's sexuality or gender identity. Rocero founded Gender Proud. Her activist group uses media to fight for transgender rights.

The Stonewall riots happened on June 28, 1969. The Stonewall Inn was a gay bar in New York City. Police raided the inn. Violence broke out. It led to 6 days of protests. It sparked the gay rights movement.

● Pride month is celebrated around the world.

On June 28, 1970, activists hosted America's first gay pride parade. They marched from Stonewall Inn to Central Park. Their official chant was, "Say it loud. Gay is proud."

Since then, activists honor the Stonewall riots in June. June is Pride month. It promotes equality. It promotes visibility of the LGBTQ+ community. It celebrates love and acceptance. It's a time to stand up for human rights.

Stand Up, Speak Out

In 1978, San Francisco hosted a Pride parade. There, the Pride rainbow flag was revealed. It became a symbol of gay pride. Artist Gilbert Baker designed the flag. Activists want to support the LGBTQ+ community. You can help!

> Celebrate Pride month. Host a Pride rainbow flag-raising ceremony. This can kick off the celebrations. Raise the flag. Make a speech. Host speakers and performances.

> Learn more about the Pride rainbow flag. Teach others about the artist. Tell others about its history and the meaning of each color. For example, red means life.

Many workplaces begin meetings by having people introduce themselves.

CHAPTER 2

USE PRONOUNS

People have the right to decide how they want to be identified. Sex is a label. At birth, people are assigned as male or female based on their **genitalia**. Genitalia are the reproductive organs. This label may not match people's gender identity. Gender identity is how people perceive themselves on the inside and what they call themselves.

We use **pronouns** as labels. Pronouns are used in place of names. Examples are he, she, and they. People should choose their own pronouns. To support LGBTQ+ folks, activists use people's pronouns. This is **affirming**, meaning strongly supporting.

Many colleges and workplaces are using pronouns. Pronoun preferences are showing up on emails too.

GET INSPIRED

BY LEGAL VICTORIES

○ In the past, many restaurants and bars refused to serve LGBTQ+ folks. The Mattachine Society protested this. This society was one of the first LGBTQ+ activist groups. On April 21, 1966, members staged a "sip-in." They went to bars all over New York City. They invited news reporters to come with them. They openly declared they were gay. They sued any place that turned them away. At the time, bars could lose their liquor license if they served gay people. It was common practice for bartenders to refuse service to openly gay men. After the sip-ins, the state's Supreme Court ruled that LGBTQ+ folks had the right to be served. The sip-in inspired other protests around the country. It inspired the opening of modern gay bars.

○ In 2015, Thailand passed the Gender Equality Act. This law banned discrimination based on sex or gender identity. It was the first Thai law to have language about LGBTQ+ folks. It inspires people to talk about LGBTQ+ issues. Activists are still fighting. They want to improve enforcement of the law.

"He" often refers to males. "She" often refers to females. For LGBTQ+ folks, these pronouns may not fit who they are. Sam Smith is a singer. Smith asked fans to call them "they/them." Smith does not want to be called "he/him." "They/them" is **gender-neutral**. This means not male or female.

Using gender-neutral pronouns creates a safe space. It shows respect. In 2019, United Airlines created new gender-neutral options. They're letting people choose the

● Instead of pronouns, some people prefer you just use their name.

title "Mx." instead of "Mr.," "Mrs.," or "Ms." When booking a ticket, passengers also have the option of marking "U" or "X" for gender. "U" is for undisclosed. "X" is for unspecified. Airlines worked with LGBTQ+ activist groups. They trained their workers to be more welcoming. They want to make flying less stressful.

● There are many pronoun options. Look them up online.

she/her • he/him • they/them • he/him • they/them • she/her

Stand Up, Speak Out

Sara is assigned female on her birth certificate. She also feels like a girl on the inside. Sara is cisgender. If you're cisgender, using pronouns may not mean much to you. But it means a lot to many LGBTQ+ folks. It increases self-love. It increases self-acceptance. Activists want to make using pronouns a regular part of life. You can help!

> Share your pronouns when meeting people.

> Ask others what their pronouns are.

> Use pronouns correctly. It's okay to make mistakes. Just apologize and try again. Practice makes perfect. This is one way to show your respect for someone's gender identity.

ALL GENDER RESTROOM

It's important to have welcoming signs in bathrooms and other spaces.

CHAPTER 3

SUPPORT GENDER-NEUTRAL BATHROOMS

In some places, there are only 2 options for public bathrooms. There's a bathroom for males. There's a bathroom for females. What if male and female labels don't work for you? LGTBQ+ folks may avoid these bathrooms. They may feel unsafe. They may feel uncomfortable. Activists want all people to have safe access to public places. They believe all people have the right to public spaces.

There are different options for making bathrooms more **inclusive** and safe. Inclusive means welcoming to all. Some businesses and cities are making all bathrooms gender-neutral. Other places are creating

GET IN THE KNOW

KNOW THE HISTORY

○ **1924** The first recorded U.S. gay rights organization formed. It was called the Society for Human Rights (SHR). It was founded by Henry Gerber. Its members started a newsletter called "Friendship and Freedom." It was the U.S.'s first gay rights publication.

○ **1998** Matthew Shepard was a gay college student in Laramie, Wyoming. He was a victim of a hate crime. People tied him to a fence, beat him, and left him for dead. He died 6 days later. Many people mourned his death and protested. Shepard's killers were sent to jail. His death led to laws against hate crimes.

○ **1999** India's first Pride parade took place. It was called the Friendship Walk. Today, it's called the Kolkata Rainbow Pride Walk. Only 15 people walked at the first parade. Now more than 20 years later, Kolkata Pride has a large following. The organization offers many events, including a queer health camp. This camp helps LGBTQ+ individuals get access to medical professionals and resources.

Title IX is a federal civil rights law. It protects people from discrimination based on sex in education. It's often used to support the rights of LGBTQ+ students.

gender-neutral bathrooms in addition to male and female bathrooms. Activists continue to push for more inclusive public spaces.

School bathrooms also need to change. Transgender students are often required to use the bathroom of their sex rather than their gender identity. This is unfair and illegal. Gavin Grimm is a transgender male. In 2014, he was 15 years old. He used the boys' bathroom at his high school. Some parents complained. Gavin was banned from using the boys' bathrooms. He sued. He said, "I just want to use the restroom in peace." In 2019 after Gavin graduated, the judge ruled in his favor. The school had violated Gavin's rights. It had to change its bathroom policy. It had to list Gavin's identity as "male" on his records. Gavin's case helped others.

● Everyone wants to feel like they belong.

Stand Up, Speak Out

In 2017, Yelp added a gender-neutral public toilet finder feature. Other companies are also trying to be more inclusive. Activists want people to stand in solidarity with LGBTQ+ folks. You can help!

> Use inclusive language. Don't say, "Hey, guys" or "Hey, ladies." Instead, use gender-neutral words. Use "folks" or "friends."

> Learn the laws. Know the laws that protect the rights of LGBTQ+ folks. Teach others. If you see anyone's rights being violated, say something.

> See if your school has a gender-neutral bathroom. If not, talk to your school leaders. Ask them to install one.

Two years after same-sex marriage became legal, more than 1 million LGBTQ+ Americans were married.

CHAPTER 4

FIGHT FOR SAME-SEX MARRIAGE

In 2004, Gavin Newsom was the mayor of San Francisco, California. He defied the U.S. law against same-sex marriage. Same-sex marriage is the marriage between 2 men or between 2 women. From February 11 to March 11, more than 4,000 gay couples were married in San Francisco. Some couples waited in line for 12 hours. There were many lawsuits. The government tried to stop San Francisco. In 2008, California made same-sex marriages legal. In 2012, President Barack Obama became the first president to publicly support same-sex marriage.

GET INVOLVED

There are several groups working to protect LGBTQ+ rights. Connect with them to get more involved.

- **GLSEN** is Gay, Lesbian, and Straight Education Network. They support LGBTQ+ students. They work to make schools a safe place. They fight against bullying.

- **HRC** is Human Rights **Campaign**. A campaign is an organized course of action. They are one of the largest LGBTQ+ support groups. They work on expanding rights for LGBTQ+ folks.

- **Lambda Legal** is a legal group. It's the first to focus on LGBTQ+ rights. Its members fight in courts. They raise awareness. They work on public policies.

- **PFLAG** is Parents, Family & Friends of Lesbians and Gays. They provide education. They help LGBTQ+ folks who are coming out.

- **The Trevor Project** serves LGBTQ+ youth. It focuses on preventing suicide. They have trained counselors to help people under age 25. They offer tools for parents and teachers.

In 2015, the U.S. Supreme Court ruled on same-sex marriage. It became legal in all 50 states.

In 2017, Bermuda made same-sex marriage legal. Then in February 2018, Bermuda banned same-sex marriage. Gay and Lesbian Alliance Against Defamation (GLAAD) is a LGBTQ+ activist group.

● In 2001, the Netherlands became the first country to legalize same-sex marriage.

It asked business and tourism leaders to speak out against the ban. People spoke out. People canceled their vacations. In June 2018, the ban was reversed. Same-sex couples are able to marry in Bermuda.

Schools should be a safe place for all students. How can you make your school safe for LGBTQ+ students?

Stand Up, Speak Out

Same-sex marriage may be legal in the United States now. But the fight isn't over. Many LGBTQ+ folks are bullied. They're abused. They feel unsafe. Some fear coming out. Activists want to change people's hearts and minds. They want to create **allies**. Allies are supporters. They support the right for LGBTQ+ folks to be who they are. You can help!

> Create safe spaces for LGBTQ+ folks. Ask to use a room at a school. Turn it into a bully-free zone. Open it to people who need a place to go.

> Be inclusive. Invite LGBTQ+ folks to hang out.

> Don't let people make LGBTQ+ jokes. Don't let people bully others. If you see something, say something.

GLOSSARY

activists (AK-tih-vists) people who fight for political or social change

affirming (uh-FURM-ing) supporting or accepting

allies (AL-eyes) supporters

boycott (BOI-kot) to refuse to buy something or take part in something as a protest to force change

campaign (kam-PAYN) an organized course of action

cisgender (sis-JEN-duhr) a person whose sex at birth matches their gender identity

gay (GAY) a person who loves a person of the same sex

gender-neutral (JEN-duhr NOO-truhl) neither male nor female

genitalia (JEN-i-TAY-lee-UH) the reproductive organs

inclusive (in-KLOO-siv) welcoming to all

justice (JUHSS-tiss) the upholding of what is fair and right

lesbian (LEZ-bee-uhn) a woman who loves another woman

pronouns (PROH-noun) words used in place of proper nouns

queer (KWIHR) a word used to describe people who identifies in a way other than straight or cisgender

strikes (STRYKES) organized protests where people refuse to do something

transgender (trans-JEN-duhr) a person whose gender expression differs from the sex they were assigned at birth

LEARN MORE!

Felix, Rebecca. #Pride: Championing LGBTQ Rights. Minneapolis, MN: ABDO Publishing, 2020.

Medina, Nico. What Was Stonewall? New York, NY: Penguin Workshop, 2019.

Pohlen, Jerome. Gay & Lesbian History for Kids: The Century-Long Struggle for LGBT Rights, with 21 Activities. Chicago, IL: Chicago Review Press, 2016.

Sicardi, Arabelle, and Sarah Tanat-Jones (illust.). Queer Heroes: Meet 53 LGBTQ Heroes from Past & Present! London, UK: Wide-Eyed Editions, 2019.

INDEX

activists/activism, 4, 5

bathrooms, 5, 6, 20–25
bisexual people, 6
bullying, 28, 31

cisgender people, 6, 19
civil rights, 23
community service, 7

discrimination, 10, 16, 23

equal rights, 10

gay people, 5, 6, 10, 16, 22
gay pride, 8–13, 22
gay pride parades, 11–12, 13, 22
gay rights movement, 11, 22

gender identity, 15, 19
Gender Proud, 11
gender-neutral bathrooms, 20–25
gender-neutral words, 17

hate crimes, 9, 22
human rights, 12

inclusivity, 21, 25, 31

Johnson, Marsha P., 10

lesbians, 5, 6, 10
LGBTQ+ activism
    community visibility, 12
    groups working to protect LGBTQ+ rights, 28
    history of, 22

legal victories, 16
pioneers in, 10
use of pronouns, 14–19
what it is, 4–7

marriage, same-sex, 26–31
Milk, Harvey, 10

Pride events, 11, 22
Pride month, 12, 13
pronouns, 14–19
public spaces, 5, 6, 21

queer people, 6

rainbow flag, 13
Rapinoe, Megan, 10

Rivera, Sylvia, 10
Rocero, Geena, 11

safe spaces, 8, 17, 21, 30, 31
same-sex marriage, 26–31
Stonewall riots, 10, 11–12
suicide, 28

Title IX, 23
transgender people, 5, 6, 10, 11, 23

violence, 8–13